Pragmatic Wisdom Vol. 3

Stoic Lessons on Living and Dying

James Bellerjeau

A Fine Idea

Contents

Chapter One

Why Do Anything? An Introduction to the Stoic Lessons

D ear friends. Join me on a journey to discover what it means to live a good life. Our inspiration in this quest is Seneca's Moral Letters to Lucilius, revisited and revised for our modern times. The search for what it means to live a good life was not new in Seneca's day, and it will not be old when we are all long gone.

Although these are not Seneca's letters, they honor both his wisdom and his instructions for new students. That is, we should grapple with deep thoughts and make our understanding of the truth personal.

Because no one has a monopoly on the truth, we can each contribute to the puzzle. **The reason to do anything is to answer a question that has not been answered, or at a minimum to answer it for yourself.**

In answering life's deepest questions, would it not be foolish for us to pass by the foundational stones laid by the great thinkers

who labored before us? Seneca himself in search of inspiration
says in his Letter 2:

> I am wont to cross over even into the enemy's
> camp, — not as a deserter, but as a scout.

Let us all be avid scouts of the great thinkers, seeking out their
every camp with the mindset of anthropologists unearthing
meaning from among the ruins. Although Seneca's words
have been mined by many for centuries, each generation keeps
turning up gemstones.

Thus, with this series of Pragmatic Wisdom for Busy People, let
us polish old stones to show them in a new light, and in washing
off the mud and debris, reveal what fresh reflections may appear.

Be well.

PS — You can read each of the volumes independently, as
it suits your time and your interests. Dedicated readers will
find, however, that their understanding of each volume will
increase upon reading further volumes. The sincere student
may therefore wish to have the full set of Stoic letters: Pragmatic
Wisdom for the Sincere Student.

Chapter Two

On the Quest for Immortality

What drives the quest for immortality? At its root, it is an excess of greed and fear

G reetings dear reader!

Your studies do you credit, and your progress will pay you dividends. For the sooner you find answers to the questions that vex you, the longer you will live in an enlightened state.

An hour spent in quiet contemplation is better than a hundred spent in confusion and so imagine the rewards for ordering your mind.

You should desire an ordered mind because you have an excellent chance at a long life. Ponder for a moment the amazing increase in life expectancy in just the last century and a half.

- In 1870, global life expectancy was a mere 29 years.

- By 2019, it had leaped to 73 years.

You would think humankind would cry out with joy at this almost tripling in our lifespan. We hear not cries of joy but lamentation.

We lament that if some have already lived to 120, why can't we all? If we can eradicate disease, if we can manipulate the very DNA that makes us what we are, can we not eliminate aging itself?

And perhaps boldest of all, if we can digitize every moment of every day, can we not simulate in our computers worlds indistinguishable from reality, and so achieve immortality, at least in code?

What drives the quest for immortality? At its root, it is an excess of greed and fear. Greed for more of what tastes sweet, for unending pleasure and consumption.

Can anything be more ill-considered? You may eat delicacy upon delicacy until your stomach groans, true. Even children soon learn gluttony comes with a price.

Radical life extensionist Ray Kurzweil himself concedes that a corporeal immortal would suffer existential ennui, running out of not only things to do but ultimately even new ideas.

Not least, achieving immortality would mean the end of humankind. If none die, none may be born. For even though we add just one per century, in an eternity an infinity would come to be. Thus, to allow eternal life means to end new life. What could be more arrogant and selfish?

All that have come before you have yielded their spot on the stage. What possible claim could we have to deny a place to all who would come after us?

"Not at all," the critics claim. "We will create all worlds digitally, all that ever were, and all that will ever be. There is space for everyone and everything." In ones and zeros, they aim to "live" forever, never growing bored or running out of new things to consume.

But nothing gains in value by being added up infinitely. As the last King of Lydia, and after conquering the Greeks, King Croesus's gold hoard was the greatest in the world, but even this was insignificant compared to what the mythical King Midas could create with a touch. Who came more to regret his lust for gold?

The value of luxury lies in scarcity; what all can possess infinitely, none will value highly in possessing.

Does the solution lie in finding some limit? Not infinity, say, but a thousand years? This would never satisfy those who fear death. Because what they fear is fear of missing out. But can anything be more foolish?

Whether your life is fifty years, one hundred, or a thousand, it shrinks in insignificance on the scale of the universe. What is a million years compared to the billions our cosmos has spun without us, and will spin on to come?

To truly avoid missing out, you would have to master not only immortality for all time yet to come but travel backward in history to sample the eternity already swallowed by time.

So, no limit can satisfy, and without limits, we destroy the value of life. The inevitable conclusion is to give up the fantasy of immortality.

By striving for what you cannot have, and would not want if you could have it, you destroy your peace of mind today.

An ordered mind knows the value of life is precisely that it is limited.

Be well.

Chapter Three

On Aging

There is no greater pleasure than being able to look back on a life of proper thoughts and actions

E verywhere I look I see signs of my own obsolescence. I cleaned out my office this week and was struck dumb by the extent to which tools I once cherished have been left to gather dust.

My HP LaserJet printer that faithfully produced thousands of pages lies beached in a corner, its power cord and printer cable laying akimbo to snare the unwary. Now my pages pass through the air wirelessly to a monster shared printer of such complexity that the architects of the moon launch must look on in wonder.

I have uncovered not less than three once miraculous devices for storing and playing my music, each compacter than the last, and concentrating more goodness into more tininess: From my first pink iPod mini to an iPod shuffle, to the iPod Nano.

Am I surprised that the next stage in development has been to shrink the iPod into invisibility, which is to say it too has become obsolete? The airwaves now carry what needed a battery, a white wire, and two earbuds to convey.

And I fairly weep to consider the fate of my most cherished guides to wisdom and universal truths: Books and printed matter.

Where once I was surrounded by reassuringly weighty volumes and binders of yellowing paper, I now see a welter of cables powering a veritable graveyard of successive e-readers.

I can mark their progress by a similar shrinking in size, though I stopped counting the generations at ten. At this rate, the population explosion we need to fear is not humankind's, but that of chips and lithium-ion batteries.

Kindle is a word that all fellow seekers of knowledge should cherish, but I admit it arouses in me now only a sense of loss. For what we have surely gained in convenience and access we have traded for competence.

The dog-eared volume, cracked spine, and underlined passages that were once the mark of the serious scholar have all given way to impermanent effervescence.

What good does it do to dip into all the libraries of the world if we do no more than browse idly for minutes before crashing on to the next electronic distraction?

I could go on chronicling the electronic wreckage, from laptops and mobile phones to rows of castaway monitors staring back at me with blank screens, but it is enough to say I am reminded that each day I am one day closer to death.

In my own case, I am not melancholy, for a purposeful life is not wasted, no matter how brief it may be.

There is no greater pleasure than being able to look back on a life of proper thoughts and actions. When you are young, everything lies before you, and you are overwhelmed by potential. What great things you are capable of, there are no limits to what you can do!

How comforting to be at the pinnacle looking back on what you have accomplished, though your journey is soon done, than to have the climb ahead of you.

And how wonderful it is to finally put an end to appetite and ambition. No more will you be goaded onwards and upwards, a donkey laboring under the stick; you now enjoy the well-deserved rest of the already done.

"Wait," you cry, "doesn't this mean you are starting to hear the stealthy footsteps that harbinger your own death?" Death does not take us in order of our age but plucks from across our ranks.

We are each of us replaced by the next generation and not only should we not resist but rejoice. I am as happy for another day as any, but I do not need it to feel fulfilled.

I bring this letter to a close.

"You do not mean," you say "to leave me hanging without a nugget of wisdom?"

Have no fear, dear reader, I bring a small offering, which packs a punch above its weight. For what is more weighty than the following words that this letter conveys:

> The man who does something under orders is
> not unhappy; he is unhappy who does something
> against his will. Let us therefore set our minds in

order that we may desire whatever is demanded of us by circumstances.

Indeed. There is no binding that can hold a person who is free in his mind.

"These are Seneca's words," you note, "and how is it that you put them to use for your own purposes here?"

I will quote Seneca and any other without end to remind us the truth belongs to us all, and not to the one who utters it.

The best ideas cannot be owned by one, only discovered and rediscovered by us all.

Be well.

Chapter Four

On Exercise Routines

Your body is a machine that deserves tending to be sure, but are you the engineer or merely a mechanic?

I t is normal to want to be fit. A sound body is a worthy goal, but your aim must be to master the body and not to become its servant.

Your fitness tracker faithfully counts your steps for you, but do you not feel its electronic whip if you falter? Many are consumed by consuming daily their avocado toast, fruit smoothie, and lean protein.

Your body is a machine that deserves tending to be sure, but are you the engineer or merely a mechanic? Do not lean too far into the role of perfect tender, lest you neglect the values that are truly dear: The vessel is not the content, no matter how fine.

When people think of fitness, it is usually only physical fitness that springs to mind.

We all know people who have entered into a holy pact with themselves to maintain the temples of their bodies. From their

Spandex shorts and functional outerwear to their latest sports watch and space-age shoes, their commitment is apparent to all.

And though it is appropriate to preserve the body, we should reserve our worship for another less visible kind of fitness: That of the mind. Mental fitness is the proper goal for the philosopher.

Lacking a solid mental foundation, the hyper-athlete is no more than fast-twitch muscles under hormonal orders. What use is it to run a marathon a month if your direction is aimless?

I will tell you, dear reader, how to keep your body in shape, without encroaching on the time and space necessary for your mental athletics.

You will recognize the truth in what I say because you have heard me say it before: Follow systems rather than goals and leverage continuous improvement principles.

Your systems are simple daily habits that you inculcate and then let run routinely, without any exercise of willpower. Feel free to walk the length of the great wall but do it a few kilometers each day as part of your normal routine.

Stock your household with nourishing food and drink, not indulgences. What comfort can you take from "comfort" food, if it leaves you steadily less fit each time you pamper yourself? You should eat to live, not live to eat.

The dedicated athlete will need all manner of supplements to maintain performance: Protein shakes to build muscle torn down by stress, electrolytes to replace salts lost to sweat, and magnesium for cramps brought on by overuse.

In both exercise and eating, you gain the most by reducing. Short, focused sessions of intense activity (high-intensity interval training), together with eating less frequently (intermittent fasting).

Your body is a most wonderful machine, capable of self-repair the best auto mechanic could only dream of. But to do its work, the body needs stillness and rest.

"Am I to lounge about," you ask, "doing nothing all day before heading to an early rest?"

Not at all, for strenuous effort is still required of the sincere student. Expend your effort, however, in being mentally strong and thinking deep thoughts.

Just as habits and routines are the keys to unlocking physical fitness, so too are they the tools for building mental strength. Establish and follow rituals in which you think, read, and write.

The more you bend your mind to following these habits, the more eagerly will your mind take to the tasks you put before it.

And because mindfulness does not require idleness, you can attend to your mental training while also going about the business of maintaining the physical machine. A meditative walk is good medicine for both the body and the soul.

I grant you now another boon, which is an insight from that most dedicated athlete of the mind and fellow Stoic, Marcus Aurelius. Let it serve as a reminder to us that all we need to successfully exercise the mind and body is within our grasp at all times:

> If you work at what is before you, following right
> reason seriously, vigorously, calmly, without
> allowing anything else to distract you, expecting
> nothing, fearing nothing, but satisfied with your
> present activity according to nature, you will live
> happy.

I wish for you to live happily, so I will extend this thought a bit further. When you expect nothing and fear nothing, it means you already have all that you need.

There is nothing that you need to attain to be successful. You may give yourself no small comfort by remembering how much you have already attained, and how this puts you ahead of the vast multitude of people on the earth.

Be grateful for what you have but be more grateful for who you are.

Be well.

Chapter Five

On Senior Citizens

If we want a true test of our training, we must check our thoughts against the one fate we can be sure is destined to come our way

I was writing not long ago about coming to terms with my ongoing obsolescence.

I fear I have left obsolescence behind and entered the realm of the antique. One still expects some functionality from the out-of-date, but the ancient is beyond function.

I have not fallen so far, so you can place me somewhere between the going and the gone.

But I am not going to complain, my dear reader, for I am still here, and you are still here. Or as the modern-day musician and author Chad Sugg put it so memorably:

> If you're reading this ... Congratulations, you're
> alive. If that's not something to smile about, then
> I don't know what is.

In my case, my essence remains, while most of my rough edges
have been worn away.

With the clamoring of youth behind me, the cares of middle
age put to rest, I am left with the companionship of an aged
but well-ordered mind. It tells me that I have earned hard-won
peace, and who am I to contradict myself?

Though I am careful not to take full credit for arranging my
thoughts in this way, because the mere passage of time does a
measure of the work for us all.

If I am perfectly happy to no longer reach for the same heights, is
it because I no longer feel the need? Or because they are beyond
my grasp?

"But," you ask, "is it not a loss to see the steadily encroaching
decline of your capabilities? To know that you will never again
do more than before, but only less?"

It is the nature of all living things to decay and die, dear reader.
I would rage as successfully against the wind as against the
inevitable decline all people face.

Let me make a claim against Lucian, whose accounts I have not
yet plundered, but whose satiric riches are available to all:

> The world is fleeting; all things pass away; or is it
> we that pass and they that stay?

That which is inevitable I am wise not only to not fear but to actively embrace.

Things that are uncertain preoccupy our minds and occupy our time. Not so the things that are certain.

If we want a true test of our training, we must check our thoughts against the one fate we can be sure is destined to come our way.

It is our habit to prepare for many things that may not come to pass, for in this way we ready ourselves not to be bothered if they do. How much more valuable the preparation for our own deaths, which should come as a surprise to no one, though we may be taken off at short or no notice.

I take comfort that my lessons have taken root. I hear them in my thoughts when no one is listening, and I feel them in my soul, which no one can touch.

Here to help pay my debts I call upon the 16th President of the United States, Abraham Lincoln who reminded us:

> It's not the years in your life that count. It's the life in your years.

I have lived, and I have no issue with either the number of my years or their nature.

And even if I was so unwise as to be ungrateful with my lot, I know that we need no more than a single day to put things right.

I am thinking of what English novelist Mary Ann Evans said, better known in her day under the name George Eliot:

It is never too late to be what you might have been.

Be well.

Chapter Six

On Reaping What Has Been Sown

For all the time that we spend worrying about things that may never happen, how much do we contemplate the one thing we can be sure of?

We pack our elderly relatives off to old folks' homes and we tell ourselves we do it so that they may be well taken care of in their dotage. Or that the burden is beyond our capabilities.

Or often, with no sense of irony, that we have no time. I suppose this last is at least true, in the sense that not one of us possesses the ability to dole out extra time to ourselves let alone another.

Our end is sealed from the beginning, dear reader, for it is the fate of all humans to perish. Rather than face this fact head-on, some hide from all hints of aging as if turning a blind eye to age can prevent it from creeping up on us unbidden.

But death is stealthy and unstoppable, part sneak thief and part mighty army, carrying away both the careless and the well-protected with equal ease. Whether you cower down in terror or stand tall in defiance, the reaper's scythe cuts as cleanly.

The question is, then, not what future awaits us, but how we await it. For all the time that we spend worrying about things that may never happen, how much do we contemplate the one thing we can be sure of?

It is one thing to dream about winning a lottery, and quite another to know with certainty that your number will be called.

Some of us fill our days with as many activities as possible as if there was a prize for getting the most things done. The more we do, though, the more we feel like we are missing out on other things we could be doing.

The American poet Stephen Dobyns put it hauntingly so:

> Each thing I do, I rush through so I can do something else. In such a way do the days pass — a blend of stock car racing and the never ending building of a gothic cathedral. Through the windows of my speeding car I see all that I love falling away: books unread, jokes untold, landscapes unvisited...

But if simply doing is not the path to joy, what is?

To contemplate an unavoidable outcome and order your mind accordingly, you must not only not look away but purposefully direct your gaze to the end.

Rather than sending off your aged parents to lonely exile, you are better served by inviting them into your life and spending your best hours with them. The benefit this will bring to them is great, but it is secondary to the benefit that accrues to your account.

Their wrinkled faces and spotted skin serve as a daily reminder of what fate holds in store for you, and that's if you are lucky. And because no outside diversion can long distract you, you are regularly encouraged to prepare yourself for the fate that awaits you.

I give you this advice freely, dear reader, and you need not subtract from my balance. Let me add to it with this contribution from Steve Jobs, whose words show he was a sincere student for the ultimate test:

> No one wants to die. Even people who want to go to heaven don't want to die to get there. And yet, death is the destination we all share. No one has ever escaped it, and that is how it should be, because death is very likely the single best invention of life. It's life's change agent. It clears out the old to make way for the new.

Now pay heed to me a little further. Preparing for the inevitable does not mean that you seek to hasten its arrival.

Though your reward is lasting peace, and freedom from all that pains you here on mortal earth, still you should not be overly hasty in concluding your journey. The point of the practice is not to desire your end, but to end your desire for life without end.

By rambling on so, I fear you will desire this letter to end before your life force is fully drained from you.

Time is allotted to us in unequal measures, and we are unevenly prepared when our measure of time is up. Think about this so that you are ready for what comes whenever it comes.

Be well.

Chapter Seven

On How All Things End

I woke up one day to see
some potion had taken its effect
and wizened my face before I
managed to bring wisdom to my
eyes

I had thought myself by now master of my senses, but I had yet another reminder today that they are still my master. For my self-possession was torn from me by something as simple as the smell of thyme in a market.

I was instantly transported to the hills of southern Spain, where herbs grow freely in the brush of the foothills cascading down from the reddish peaks to the Mediterranean.

And your face, my dear reader, was just as quickly before me recalling to mind the hikes we took with the family up and down those rocky ravines among those hardy herbs.

It seems we were just there together, basking in the buildup of afternoon heat and languishing through days where the sunlight never seemed to fade.

In my memories, time becomes a disordered jumble. I can pluck a scene from my pre-teens that feels as near in time to me as other dramas that played out when my own children were that age.

My parents never seemed to age, frozen in one unchanging state, but time's invisible passage has left its visible marks upon them.

Now I have aged myself, though I similarly did not note time's magic as it worked upon me. I woke up one day to see some potion had taken its effect and wizened my face before I managed to bring wisdom to my eyes.

Though these memories in my mind tell me that everything is yet as it was, I need but look around me to see that my internal map has not kept up with the landscape:

- Shall I count the number of gravestones bearing silent witness to the fact that the ranks of our comrades have been thinned by death's scythe?

- Not many of these were taken in their prime, and what does that say about how stealthily time lulls us into submission?

I look up and see buildings gone, entire blocks upheaved and remade, cities that bear the same name but whose streets I do not know by heart, like the goat paths we used to tread as children.

At this rate, can we doubt that the very mountains we once clambered up will be gradually worn down and themselves swept into the sea?

Some get so swept up in the course of their campaigns that they consider only current affairs and give no thought to what brought them to that pass, or in which direction they are heading.

In my case, I cannot say that I was unaware while events unfolded, for mindfulness has been my practice for many a year.

- I recall my decision to study law after abandoning the pursuit of the study of the mind (how light a decision for something that would prove so weighty over my life!),

- meeting the love of my life in law school (though the vision of her distracted me mightily from my lessons!),

- the rites of passage accompanying my passing the bar (what a low bar it now seems for such a high pursuit, and would that we set it much higher to maintain the rule of law!), and

- the joy at turning my love of words into the otherwise laborious practice of law (how something so pure can be turned into something so base when every principle comes with a price tag attached!).

No, dear reader, in my head I am still in all of these states simultaneously: Chomping at the bit to start the race, undisciplined and prodigious in my expenditure and waste of energy, finding my easy rhythm and stride, one day rearing up accomplished and experienced, then at one moment first noticing the load I was pulling, and now feeling the full weight of that load inexorably slowing me to a halt.

The more I have accomplished, the more I find myself looking backward rather than looking forward.

I tell myself this is only natural, and moreover, it is the correct course because no lesson is as well learned as the one you have taught yourself. But this introspection also gives me pause, because I realize time never pauses for us.

We are but poor judges of time, for we never once correctly estimate that time's passage is the same for us all and is the same at all times.

- In our childhood we are heedless, and this makes time seem endless.

- In our youth we are reckless, and this makes us wasteful of time.

- In our middle age, we take note and start to enjoy the finer notes of life and time.

- And as we approach the finish line, we are alarmed, for we realize the race we've been rushing through awards a prize that none would jump the line to receive early.

Knowing finally that every hour contains but sixty minutes, and every minute but sixty seconds, each moment seems infinitely more precious to us precisely because we know they are slipping through our fingers, never to return.

What irony that it takes a lifetime to learn that we should take none of our lives for granted!

If it was in my power to change just one part of the human condition, I would make memory work in both directions. That is, let us remember our futures as clearly as we do our pasts.

If as youths we could call to mind not just the small number of things already done, but the vast number yet to come, we would realize the fullness of life as it is happening, rather than after it has passed.

Be well.

Chapter Eight

On Knowing Your Limits

Awkwardness, thy name is Smalltalk!

I f you are looking to convince me of your latest pet theory, dear reader, you should make the attempt now, for I was recently convinced to once again attend a social dinner.

It was an honor to be invited; the attendees counted select law school faculty and local legal luminaries. The occasion was a lecture arranged by the Europa Institut, and if I should manage to stick to the public portion of these events I would be a happy man.

I was drawn from my solitude, lured once again by the outstanding quality of the speaker, though I knew well what giving in to this temptation would entail:

- the pre-talk private meet and greet, presenting a chance to shake hands and perhaps get a favorite volume signed; and even more enticingly,

- the post-talk dinner for invited guests, and the forced

intimacy that comes from assigned seating.

No, I will not say which event it was, because that would not be fair to any of the participants. Suffice it to say there are few opportunities indeed for one such as me to be put face to face with Ambassadors, Federal judges, and even Justices of the United States Supreme Court.

Perhaps to the layperson, the names Alito, Ginsberg, and Scalia call to mind only thoughts of vague European heritage, but to the constitutional lawyer, they are blazing stars in the night sky.

"Sounds delightful," you say, "and yet I detect a hint of complaint. What am I missing?"

Truly I am an ungrateful wretch, but I will tell you that these events make me wretched, for all that I cannot stay away.

Imagine how you would feel meeting a genuine inspiration, a hero whose works you have studied and admired from afar. My stomach flutters and my intestines are tied in knots. Prone to sweating from the lightest of exertions, I become a sticky mess affixed to my place by the buffet table.

To avoid acting a fool and not just looking like one, I raise my glass and join the toast. The last thing my gut needs is food and drink, which just roils my belly much as my thoughts and emotions are already roiled.

Social trivialities in the presence of such weighty people and ideas seem the greatest waste to me, but I never seem to navigate safely the path between banalities or a boring inquisition on something significant but out of place in this setting.

Awkwardness, thy name is Smalltalk!

And to know that I will inflict myself on an unwitting dinner table with my unwitty remarks makes me wish most fervently to return to my hermit's cave.

I venture forth each time for the same reason, dear reader: Nowhere else are the chances better of hearing unvarnished truth and wisdom.

These speakers and judges are at the peak of their careers, brimming with knowledge, experience, and insight. They are also typically near the *end* of their careers, and because Federal judges are appointed for life, this means they are near the end of their lives.

I've often thought the invitation to speak at these series is like an advance copy of one's obituary. Considering how many have passed away not long after speaking, I'd be superstitious about not passing up an invitation to speak.

They have gained confidence because of their age and experience. More importantly, they've typically gained wisdom, not least in having learned not to care what other people think.

Consider what happens if you are presented daily for decades with opposite sides of every issue and forced to decide which is correct, or whether neither is correct and a third way is appropriate.

This will make you very good at deciding, and to stay sane you must also believe you are making good decisions. Remember, at the level of the Supreme Court there is no further appeal, so yours is the last voice.

For us to hear such learned people speak their minds without regard to what others think, and with neither the intent to flatter nor offend, is a rare blessing.

Philosophy holds out this blessing to each of us, without the agony of gilded invitations to pre-talk toasts or post-talk parties: The chance to hear and understand the unvarnished truth, for any whose eyes and ears are open to the message.

Yes, it is uncomfortable to be confronted with one's failings and frailties. To not look away because there is no hiding from oneself, no higher court to take up the appeal.

But to admit a weakness is to put a name and a face to that weakness, which is the first critical step to overcoming it and becoming stronger.

Philosophy helps us not because it tells us that we are perfect, but in holding up a mirror to our faults. By helping us recognize our limitations we can most profitably direct our efforts to where we need them most.

Are you warned to be wary of wants? Then pay attention to the signs indicating you are wanting more than you need.

Are you plagued by worry over what other people think? By ordering your mind to understand the true nature of things you learn that ignorant opinions carry no weight and so should not burden you.

Philosophy ultimately arms us against all that ails us, but we must first let her indicate that we are ill.

Be well.

Chapter Nine

On Existence and Its Opposite

What does it say if you cannot say you are living today, but only preparing for a tomorrow that may never come?

Are you happier knowing the instrument of your end, or remaining ignorant of it?

Though we are at the peak of health and can complain of no ailment, still we carry the seeds of our end with us at all times.

- Accidents carry some away in their prime, and the one consolation is that the end comes quickly.

- Cancer can strike at any age, and its cruelty is a lingering finish.

Imagine the feeling that not just a general end at a future time but a specific doom hangs over you.

For some, getting notice of a terminal illness is a death sentence to their happiness. "All that I could have done, would have done, want to do!"

What a pity that they ruin the remaining life they have because they do not have longer to live. For consider, there is not one of us who could not be carried off today.

What does it say if you cannot say you are living today, but only preparing for a tomorrow that may never come? What does it say if you cannot be happy today unless you think you will be around to be happy tomorrow?

I say it is a blessing to be confronted with our mortality, dear reader, and that it should not only not make us morbid, but rather joyful for what we have.

Knowing that your time is limited, do you not value it more highly than if your days were to run into each other to eternity?

If you find your perspective still lacking, consider the relative flicker that is human existence compared to the broad sweep of time.

- Whether you live a year, a decade, or a century, you are but a pinprick on the long ribbon of unfurling time.

- You missed all that came before you came into existence, but did you suffer any pangs or pains for your loss? You did not, because you were not.

- Will you suffer after you are gone? I believe not, because you will not be.

You will recognize me as carving onto the page here the Epicurean epitaph:

Non fui, fui, non-sum, non-curo (I was not, I was, I am not, I do not care).

Our existence is but the briefest moment, dear reader. See to it that you do not merely exist.

Order your mind so that it neither dwells too long in the past nor resides chiefly in the future. Stretch too far in either direction, and you will anyway be among the non-existent.

The ordered mind comes about from choosing your state of mind. You cannot be compelled to do anything that you do willingly.

So whatever your circumstance is at the moment, make a game of turning an unexpected turn to your favor.

What seems to be your worst luck can also be your best luck, if you simply turn the frame of reference in the right direction.

- Your train is late? You have more time to listen to the birds and feel the sunshine on your face.

- Oh no, it's started raining! You now have an unscheduled demonstration of your hardiness to inconveniences.

- Your flight is cancelled? You have just won an unplanned holiday and a chance to experience a new city first-hand.

"These are but trivialities," you say. "Do you really expect me to be happy in the face of serious misfortune?"

I do expect it, for your own sake I do, and I urge you to think about it now.

- Your job is eliminated? This gives you the opportunity to get away from annoying colleagues and start that side business you've been dreaming of.

- Your doctor returns holding your x-rays and says "We have to talk" in a grim intonation? You will soon have the uncertainty of your end cleared up, and all the burdens and struggles and pains and worries will be eased from your shoulders. Others will carry on and carry the load for you.

There is a distinction I would have you learn. To accept your end cheerfully does not mean you seek to hasten its arrival.

Would you consider a man wise who, upon spying a $100 bill at his feet, walks on by, saying "I do not need it." Only the foolish spurn what is on offer, just as the wise eagerly receive that which others would push away.

The distinction is that you learn not to want what you cannot have, and to appreciate and value what you *do* have.

Just because you do not need good health, wealth, and long life to be happy, you do not give them up to demonstrate your independence from them.

I must end now, and take my leave. Before I go, I leave you with this summary: to know your specific end is to know that we all must end, but no one said we need to end in tears.

Be well.

Chapter Ten

On Living a Full Life

We tell ourselves we'll be happy if only we can achieve something else. But this treadmill only speeds up the faster we run

Let us stop behaving as if we are living a dress rehearsal and can fix our lines and redo our actions tomorrow.

This has been my singular aim for some time now, dear reader. I do not assume I will have more time, that I will be able to complete later all that I have left unfinished today.

- I tell myself this may be the last breakfast I will enjoy.

- I am writing as if this was my last letter.

- My son is off to work, my daughter about her studies, and my spouse on the way to the grocery store, and do I tell myself we may never see each other again?

You may think such thoughts would train one to be melancholy, but in my experience, they foster tranquility and joy.

Reflecting on the scarcity of the present makes it seem infinitely precious to me.

The past is gone, and may it stretch out emptily for eons behind us for all the good that it will do us today. To live in the past is not to live at all.

Look to the future then! But the future may never arrive, and by casting my thoughts ahead I rob the present of my watchful presence.

We put things off for two reasons: we don't want to do them at all, or we *do* want to do them but we assume we'll get to them later.

In putting off that which we dread, do we assume we'll be more successful than the ostrich in avoiding troubles? When we raise our heads from the sand, will we find our unpleasant tasks have gone away, or have only multiplied in our self-imposed blindness?

Learn this lesson dear reader, and you will live a happy life: Tell yourself that you do nothing against your will; that though the task may be strenuous or unpleasant it is done by your own choosing.

You do not dread that which you do willingly. So no matter the chore, put yourself fully behind it and you will be successful regardless of the outcome.

The temptation to put off supposed burdens is at least understandable. But why do so many put off living joyfully in fulfillment? Isn't that the goal we're striving towards?

We tell ourselves we'll be happy if only we can achieve something else. But this treadmill only speeds up the faster we run.

The only sensible course is to step off the treadmill, to step off and take stock of all you have at this immediate moment.

It sounds trite, but you can be satisfied today if you only set aside disappointment — just as you choose your actions, choose your attitude and you will be similarly successful.

If you assume your time is limited to today, you will waste less of it and enjoy more of it.

Be about the business of living, then, and live each day fully, and you will not be troubled by either the past or the future.

Be well.

Chapter Eleven

On the Proper Measure of Grief

If you would treasure your times with true friends, you will every now and then permit yourself to imagine life without them

Your friend J. has succumbed in his battle with cancer, and we mourn. You are right to be sad, but I would have you avoid turning a pure thing into a selfish thing by mourning to excess.

If I were to tell you that you should not mourn at all, you would think me to be asking too much, although in truth you'd be better for it.

But it takes a person of rare self-possession to be above all bother about what occurs on the mortal plane. Even such an elevated person would note the passing of a dear friend, but their noting would not turn into a drawn out dirge.

In our case we may let our sorrow show, so long as we can then show that we have let it go.

You do not need to harden your heart to feeling strong emotions. That is not what I am advising.

You need merely observe the cries and carrying on that accompany the bereaved, though, to be warned of over-acting.

"Acting," you say, "are my feelings for my friend not genuine?"

I do not doubt your feelings are real, dear reader, but consider whether they are well-placed, and, equally, well-timed.

Some people seek to demonstrate the depth of their feeling by the depth of the tears they shed upon a loved one's passing. Too often this is a display for the benefit of the living, to prove as it were, that their feelings were real.

Were their feelings as intense when their friend was still among us? Did they lavish attention on their friend as they now lavish it on their grief?

We take for granted what is all around us, losing moments to hours, then hours to years, to inattention and neglect.

"I will see him next week sometime. I am busy with other things, and I don't have time for him today."

Only when we have lost them forever do some start to appreciate and value those we had with us all along. In such cases, our grief should be real, but it is grief for ourselves having wasted valuable parts of our time with others.

And what of the one who says they are inconsolable? None of their living, loving friends will do, because of the one who is gone.

A friend who puts the dead above the living deserves no friends among the living. Because if you know the true worth of your friends you will value their words of comfort.

And if you say you have no friends who understand you, then you have little understanding of yourself or others.

Do you think you are alone in feeling lonely, feeling sad, feeling lost? Do you think that none has suffered an unfairness or injury before you?

The conditions of mankind's existence are such that, though blessings are spread unevenly, suffering is widely shared. To think you are uniquely suffering is to risk adding arrogance to ignorance.

There are multiple ways to prepare yourself against the pain of loss of companionship:

- You can reflect on and savor the good moments as they are happening, and so build up a store of memories that will last as long as you do;

- You can build up reserves in your relationships, in the form of multiple friendships; and

- You can anticipate the end of all things, including your loved ones, not in dread and fear, but in simple acknowledgment that all things end.

Time you spend mindfully with your friends leaves a lasting impression.

You are not only listening but hearing. You are not only talking but being heard and understood. The laughter that arises spontaneously represents a shared joy.

You may revisit this treasure-house of memories at your leisure, when you are merely temporarily parted from your friends, or when they are permanently taken from us.

How would you have your friends remember *you*?

With this thought in mind, make it your habit to build memories of your current interactions so that you have good times to act as a bulwark against the bad.

When you are at peace with yourself, you make it easier for others to interact honestly with you.

You may teach without judging. You may observe without criticizing.

We think we want praise, but in our hearts, we know that flattery is a compliment that makes one uglier over time.

Be a good friend, and you will find friends.

Fortune can be fickle indeed, but having friends you can count on counts for a lot. You will then have companions to understand and share your feelings when one of you is taken out of order.

If you would treasure your times with true friends, you will every now and then permit yourself to imagine life without them.

Not to make yourself sad by hastening or even bringing about the loss, but to remind yourself never to assume too much. If you are aware that every parting could be your last, you will hold the embrace that much longer.

The casual "See you later," betrays an unthinking optimism that creates the conditions for bitter disappointment. If you never expect other than to see your loved ones again, of course, you will be grieved if they are taken away.

Better to think and to say "We may never meet again, dear friend. I am happy for the times we had together. Take care."

It is with sorrow, but not grief, that I bring this letter to a close.

I rejoice for the time we have spent together, dear reader, and you are never far from my thoughts and memories. I am happy to extend our time together through our correspondence.

For even though we do not meet, something is better than nothing, and in this case that something is everything to me.

Be well.

Chapter Twelve

On the Will To Live

The legal profession has found a way to work true magic: that is, they can speak for the dead

Today the sun is shining and everywhere Spring is in evidence. Fragrant blossoms perfume the air and please the eyes with vibrant bursts of color that stand out among rich fields of green. Life returns, refreshed and revitalized after its winter lull and pause!

And yet, not every sprig has sprouted. The blueberry bushes my wife and I transplanted have seen their numbers reduced by a fifth, bare stems reminding us that life is also precious and fickle.

Was it a nick of the shovel, a few too many rocks blocking the roots, or water that failed to flow when needed? The gardener and farmer take life the least for granted because they know what conditions it requires to flourish as well as how easily it can slip away.

Much of philosophy, dear reader, and certainly a great deal of Stoic writing, is concerned with what it means to live a good life.

What are the pursuits that give life meaning, and how should we conduct ourselves during our lives?

The Stoics believed that a person should become a gardener tending their own well-ordered mind so they could live their lives according to reason. This meant applying reason to every sort of situation, positive or negative, and behaving according to reason rather than the unthinking passions of the moment.

Living well thus also meant contemplating the end of life and dying well. Have you noticed how many topics people today consider inappropriate for polite conversation?

Consider: We are all bound for one and the same destination. Though we usually delight in sharing every detail of our planned vacations, this is one pending trip that remains an open secret, known by all but unmentionable.

Yes, we're all traveling there together, but if you mention it, you are as welcome as the dog who drags a dead woodchuck into the living room. Better that you actually raise the dead than raise the specter of thinking of death and let zombies loose on our imaginations.

The Stoics understood that wanting things and fearing things prevents people from living in peace. Because wanting and fearing are conditions of the mind, the thought goes, mastering the mind provides the key to contentment.

If fear of death disrupts the good life, then it must be confronted. I fear that in modern society we have completely lost the lessons and the practices of the ancients and have turned things on their heads.

We have surrendered fully to the pursuit of more: More things, more life, more experiences. When we know from the evidence daily before our eyes that *more* is no guarantee of *better*.

We close our minds to things that are unpleasant to think of, as if merely shutting our eyes could make the danger disappear.

"Where does our willful blindness come from? Why have we forgotten that what is limited is precious, and quantity alone is no guarantee of quality?"

I put the blame at the feet of two of our oldest professions: First, doctors, about whom more in a moment; and second, those purveyors of hourly pleasure, selling themselves to the highest bidder without regard for the person purchasing their services.

I speak of lawyers, about whom also more in a moment, though you may prefer less of them.

Doctors have progressed far beyond the alchemy of their early days. Their collective progress in prolonging life has made some into mad scientists, pushing the boundaries of life extension outward, outward.

There is no part of the human body that we will not repair, cut out, or replace if it means the machine can be kept ticking. No part, that is, except the soul and the mind, which stubbornly resist being duplicated by our best 3-D printers.

"What," you say, "would you have our medical professionals forget their Hippocratic Oath? They are bound by millennia of ethics to not only 'do no harm or injustice' to their patients, but also not to administer poison though asked, or to suggest it be taken."

I say keep reading the Oath, my dear reader, for the following words are misinterpreted by many today:

> Into whatsoever houses I enter, I will help the sick, and I will abstain from all intentional wrong-doing and harm, especially from abusing the bodies of man or woman.

Does it really help the incapacitated or terminally ill to extend by any means their stay on earth for so long as our mad scientists can manage?

- Can it ever be intentionally wrong to shock a heart back into beating, after the manual massage of cardiopulmonary resuscitation has failed?

- Is it always a help to keep a body breathing by mechanical ventilator after the will to breathe no longer comes from within?

- Can it not be abuse to force feed a body by intravenous tube when all desire to eat has fled?

We ourselves might make a different decision were it our own body lying on the table, but the patient who cannot make a decision at all is assumed to always want more: Keep the fluids in my body flowing, hook me up to every machine, spare no expense in my maintenance!

Though the patient may have been a little lax in their own preventative care, we assume that they mean for others to move mountains to now make up for their neglect.

But how inconsistent we are when it comes to choosing the manner of our deaths! The one who is mute is assumed to ask for every aid. Yet the ones who have their faculties intact and their individual agency at hand put their powers to killing themselves and others with abandon.

Consider that most of the deaths in the U.S. today count our own behavior as primary or contributing causes: Heart disease, respiratory diseases, stroke, and diabetes.

It is not blaming the patient to note that a healthy weight and diet, and an active lifestyle, help prevent or mitigate many chronic conditions.

Cancer is near the top of death's choice of weapons, and while it is an indiscriminate killer, some versions are certainly courted by their victims, if not downright invited in to dance.

(And this does not even count the intentional deaths, those actively sought out, of which abortion would be the silver medalist on the podium were we to include it in the statistics for causes of death. We do not count abortion because the unborn do not count. I am not arguing the point about when life begins. I observe merely that murder, suicide, and execution represent but small figures compared to what happens to the unborn, who themselves are least able to express their wishes.)

How and why did this come to pass, dear reader? Why did we need government accountants to invent the quality-adjusted life year or QALY to tell us that we can determine the economic value of medical interventions by measuring both the quality and the quantity of life lived?

That a year lived in perfect health is worth more than one lived in pain and ill health, and indeed that some health states can be considered "worse than dead"?

Well, let me speculate on a possible reason.

If the medical profession has transcended alchemy to arrive at a practice more resembling science, the legal profession has found a way to work true magic: That is, they can speak for the dead.

To that short list of things that can be guaranteed in life (death and taxes), we can add a third: Lawsuits. No accident, no death, no act, no inaction, no treatment, but that a lawyer will be standing by to take the case.

A tort claim has only a few ingredients: Duty, breach, cause, and harm.

- Doctors more than most professionals owe a duty to their patients. Did we not just recite sections of the Hippocratic Oath, proof of what we intuitively understand?

- If the patient suffers an adverse outcome in a doctor's care, a lawyer can easily argue all the other elements of negligence: There must have been some failure (breach), and without it (cause) my client would not have died (harm).

Aristotle could have been describing the plight of doctors practicing modern medicine when he said:

> There is only one way to avoid criticism: Do nothing, say nothing, and be nothing.

This condition leads to predictable outcomes: A strong bias to seek the preservation of life at all costs. I may raise the costs of your care exponentially, but that is less expensive to me than getting sued for failing to pursue a possible treatment. So, you will be kept alive whether you want it or not.

At least in part, it is lawyers speaking for the dead who drive such interventions. But when patients are free to speak for themselves, they are considerably less concerned about extending life in all circumstances.

The explosion of living wills and advance directives is proof that laypersons know what professionals do not: We do not want to live forever if it means our quality of life is ignored.

Everyone draws the line differently. Ease my pain with palliative care, but do not perform extraordinary measures. Do not resuscitate, intubate, or ventilate.

No matter how much people close their eyes to the consequences of their daily decisions and conveniently ignore that they will one day have to pay the bill for their lavish expenditures, still I think many instinctively know that their end can be of their choosing.

The will to live does not always serve you best by driving you to seek more.

You may find that you achieve a better life by virtue of contemplating the end of your life and working backward from that point to living a meaningful life.

Be well.

Chapter Thirteen

On Our Duty To Live

While we have breath in the body, we must not give up. Not because we fear death, nothing so mundane. But because we can do good in the world by living

You have tested positive for COVID, dear reader, and surely this is unwelcome news! Although be thankful that you have experienced thus far no more than a headache and a fever that abated after 24 hours.

It is true that many have contracted the virus without even knowing it and only discover later that they have the antibodies coursing through their veins. But others are laid low out of proportion to any pre-condition or co-morbidity, and of these, some have perished.

We have lost family, friends, and strangers to this discriminating killer. We think we are gaining the upper hand with our vaccines, but the mystery of why some are so afflicted while others remain unaffected is unsolved.

We who remain among the living are left to ponder the mystery of life as much as that of death. The latter is inevitable, it is just a question of time, what will carry you off and not whether. A good life, on the other hand, is something that some never attain no matter how long they live.

It is not the affliction of disease that necessarily prevents one from living a meaningful life according to reason. More often it is afflictions of the mind that leave the untrained stricken. And yet it is the mind that has the power to diminish, if not to fully heal, many an illness of body and soul.

The mind can transport us to worlds far removed from our present discomfort and pain. A moving song arouses a deep stirring within our breast, a captivating movie can make us forget our common cares for a few hours.

For me, it is the written word that most easily and most completely steals me away. I forget to eat, the hours slip by like minutes, and I become a master builder of cathedrals in the sky.

These castles are airy, but still, they have substance in my mind, and I am as convinced by the solidity of their walls as if I were rapping the cold stone against my knuckles. In these states, corporeal concerns lose essence and dissipate.

My hangover upon returning to reality is to realize I am human, ridiculous in my wants and desires, fragile and easy to damage. The gradual replication errors in my personal computer code compound and cumulate until I am but a single free radical away from cancer finding its origin in a once healthy cell.

Despite our fragility, in fact I would say *because* of it, we have a duty to persevere. For if we are vulnerable despite all the armor we have learned to take up and deploy in response to countless challenges, how much do our fellow travelers suffer, who are less protected and do not even know why they suffer?

Confucius tells us that a child who honors their parents will demonstrate filial piety. Specifically, he says:

> There is filial piety when parents are spared all anxiety about their children except when they happen to fall sick.

Do we think it is only us who suffer when we are ill and take no cure? Our family, our friends, and most of all our parents, are each given to suffer when we stumble about blindly in pain, in addiction, and in misery.

So, to start we shall be dutiful children to our parents and honor their sacrifices in bringing us into the world and teaching us to the best of their ability.

We shall do this by not giving them cause to be anxious about our condition. If we are unhealthy, we shall accept the help that is offered, we shall seek out the cures that are available, and we shall above all *help ourselves*.

Every person has in them the ability to aid or hinder their cure.

"What patient does not willingly, gladly, take the medicine that would heal them?" you ask.

An astonishingly large number of the unwell, dear reader, reject advice, defy treatment, and punish themselves with further decay. For the sake of our parents, we must be model patients. For encouragement, call to mind the words of the Buddha, who tells us:

> You yourself, as much as anybody in the entire universe, deserve your love and affection.

This is just the start. For what kind of friend are we if we incapacitate ourselves of the ability to be of support to them? For surely, they suffer just as we do.

If we are of sound mind and healthy body, we can assist them in their difficult times. Not because that means they are in a position to help us when we need a helping hand, but simply because that is what it means to be a friend: To give freely and willingly what you are able when you are able.

And if we must heal ourselves to help our friends, those few carefully cultivated from among thousands, how much more potential good can we do if we make ourselves available to the many?

They are none of them asking for our help, true. They do not even know we exist. But we know that *they* exist, and we know that they suffer, as surely as our friends and family do. Are they not our sisters and brothers in humanity?

What does it say if I let this brother fall by the trail and leave that sister hungry and thirsty because I have turned away and not spent the time to know them? If we but spoke a few sentences, we would know the truth of our shared burdens and our shared humanity.

The well-ordered mind following reason is content in itself, but this does not mean that it is cut off from the rest of humankind or that it seeks isolation.

The gurus who secrete themselves away in caves may be sufficient to themselves, but they are insufficient for any purpose other than serving as examples.

To some, they are an example of how to attain lasting peace. If that peace comes at the cost of sharing the burdens of humanity, I say they are rather an example of how to make selfishness a virtue. Everyone can help someone, but to help *only* yourself is to help no one.

Thus, we have a duty to live, dear reader, to will ourselves well when we are ill. While we have breath in the body, we must not give up.

Not because we fear death, nothing so mundane. But because we can do good in the world by living; we can make the world a better place by our presence.

We do not diminish ourselves by giving of ourselves, we only increase the stock of goodness in the world. I end with the kind words of the Buddha once more today, for his wisdom still rings true:

> Thousands of candles can be lighted from a single candle, and the life of the candle will not be shortened. Happiness never decreases by being shared.

Be well.

Chapter Fourteen

On Training To Improve

The side effects of not only being physically fit, but training to become and remain physically fit, are certainly real

T he best thing you can say about the physical fitness craze, the best thing, is that inadvertently some will come to greater peace of mind by virtue of their training.

The side effects of not only being physically fit but training to become and remain physically fit, are certainly real. This is the case even though these benefits are rarely the original purpose for one's taking up the training.

"What are these inadvertent benefits of pursuing a course of physical fitness?" you ask.

Here are some examples that come to my mind. First, we learn how to form habits by observing that the things we repeatedly do become easier after just a short interval of repetition. How valuable to discover that we are not only or even primarily creatures of will, but creatures of habit!

The expenditure of will is only necessary to start us off. Once well begun we will continue on our course like a Newtonian particle continues in its direction unless acted upon by another force.

Next, we learn how to overcome adversity by enduring the inevitable strains we encounter in our physical pursuits. We learn that emerging victorious makes us yet more capable.

- Lifting weights puts stress on our muscles, creating small tears and cellular destruction that, upon healing, grow back stronger.

- Running and sprinting wears out our legs, but in return builds our ability to process oxygen and improves the heart's efficiency for all the remaining time we are at rest.

- Bicycling long distances taxes our tender behinds as much as it toughens our capacity for boredom.

- Swimming teaches us our skin is largely impervious to water, and that if we can only keep our mouths shut at the right times and in the right rhythm, we can be surrounded by otherwise fatal environments and emerge unharmed.

- Stretching and yoga remind us that our bodies are also machines and that it is both necessary and wonderful to periodically pause the abuse we inflict in order to lovingly maintain and care for them.

Finally, in pursuing a measured course of physical fitness, we greatly enhance our chances of living our lives free from avoidable ailments.

No diet or exercise can protect us from all dangers, though many convince themselves otherwise, but there are countless self-imposed chains of disease and ill health that the healthy specimen has broken and cast aside.

Do you ask me now if it is also a good thing that healthy habits may also lead to longer lives? Here I am more reserved in my praise, dear reader. A longer life can be a blessing, true, but living long by no means ensures that one lives well.

For all the benefits I have just listed, there are many things much less flattering that we must lay at the feet of a focus on physical fitness.

For one, how many mistake fitness itself for the end, rather than a means to an end? For another, the positive reinforcement generated by a focus on the body means it risks becoming one's sole focus. This in turn prevents attention to the much more pressing task of training the mind.

If we are constantly struggling to be physically fit, how many more struggle to be *mentally* fit when they do not even know that as much training is necessary for the mind, if not more, to stay healthy?

If we spent a tenth of the time obsessing about our state of mind as we did the numbers on our fitness tracker, we could be confident in saying all were on their way to well-ordered minds. But just as the pool is not the best environment for deep conversation, the modern-day environments we immerse ourselves in are not conducive to the habit of reflection.

Consider first what is on offer to the budding athlete in pursuit of a healthy body. The cyclist has a range of bicycles on display in ever lighter and more exotic materials, at prices ranging from the expensive to the shocking to the unconscionable. Compared to this, the helmet, shoes, lighting, lock, padded shorts, and reflective jacket are but pricy insults, annoying but far from the greatest harm.

The runner secretly laughs because they need nothing more than the open road and a pair of sneakers, right? Nike is having the last laugh here when they ring in the sales from lightweight sneakers that combine carbon plates, foam, and micro-weave into a package so light that they are worth their weight in gold.

And this is to say nothing of water-wicking socks, functional shorts, and odor-repelling microbial-infused shirts. Oh, it's cold today! Another jacket or two will ease your discomfort. What's that? Rain, you say? No worries, wear this hat and that jacket, and you're right as rain.

Sunny tomorrow? These prescription sunglasses will wrap around your head and block wind and stray light; look we have lenses for bright days, for foggy days, for forest paths, and even for nighttime journeys. Wrap your head around all the costs the runner faces, dear reader, and you will no longer pity the biker.

I myself would be embarrassed to tell you how much I have spent on successive generations of GPS trackers from the likes of Polar and Garmin. I can regale with you far more details than merely my precise location! My heart rate, steps, speed, and cadence.

Do you want to know the altitude, how long I slept and how deeply, the interval between my heartbeats, or whatever the delightfully named VO2Max will tell you about me? Before I've figured out the hundreds of functions on my current watch of wonder, another has come along with even more features, at an even greater price.

Yet for all the thousands I've spent on watches now collecting dust and not data, I would spend all this and more if someone offered a device that could tell me not just where I was on the earth, but why I was there. Can Garmin tell me if the direction I am heading is the right one, or am I just running in circles?

I could go on in this vein, but because I know your thoughts and I am kind, I will not.

Let me observe instead that among the thousands of offerings focused on the body's function, I suppose we should take heart that there has emerged a handful dedicated to what is within our heads.

Headspace comes to mind, with its laudatory mission of helping cultivate the practice of mindfulness. The ills being treated here are not those of the body, but rather things like sleep, stress, loneliness, regret, anxiety, and more.

Though it is too soon to say whether their offering is mere pabulum or manna for the mind, I am encouraged simply by the fact that this ancient art of training exists in a new form that makes it appealing to the masses.

In this instance, I welcome the madness of crowds and the folly of following fads. Even though it may be uncritical mob behavior that drives the growth in mindfulness practice, still it is the practice of the mind. Can we not expect practitioners to harvest inadvertent benefits regardless of their motivations?

Every day remind yourself that your most important function for living is your mind, and your body is more a vessel for carrying it about.

When you have the hierarchy of things in the right order, you will find it easier to devote the time to training your mind and not just your body.

Be well.

Chapter Fifteen

On the Utility in Catastrophe

People fall too readily into the habit of taking their lives for granted and this in turn leads them away from living their lives meaningfully and well

M any rail against the dark turn our media has taken. It seems they delight in arousing our anger and our emotions. They monetize our fear by keeping us hooked to our screens.

I tell you that rather than cursing the media, the modern philosopher should be giving them thanks. We shall thank them for these daily reminders of our frailty as humans in an unforgiving world.

If we kept a statistician by our side, we would know to walk more carefully under the branches of the trees in our neighborhood than we would think to duck our heads in worry about space debris from a Chinese rocket falling to earth.

If we were as facile with numbers as we are comfortable conjuring images in our heads, we would more eagerly step into an airplane than we would hop in our cars for the drive to work each morning. But things that fall from the sky are so much more interesting!

We cannot look away, and so they capture our imagination and make hostages of our reason.

But for just a moment, my dear reader, let us welcome the media whipping our irrationality to new heights.

- A shark has mistaken a surfer for a seal and taken a bite? Delightful!

- A lightning bolt has determined that the shortest route to ground lies through a hiker's head? Fascinating!

- A person has found a novel way to misuse a product and so slices, eviscerates, or defenestrates themselves? Most excellent!

Now it is not my aim to mock misfortune or tragedy, for though rare these instances are very real, not least to their chomped, electrified, and impaled victims. I take no delight in the suffering of others.

"So why," you ask, "did you just say we should welcome the news of these events?"

The explanation is this. People fall too readily into the habit of taking their lives for granted and this in turn leads them away from living their lives meaningfully and well.

If the misfortune of others serves to jolt us from our sleepwalking, then each of these dark clouds does indeed hold a silver lining.

The scope of human suffering is broad, and we need not limit our contemplation to these instances of isolated injury. The COVID pandemic is a powerful reminder that we are surrounded by pathogens and that sometimes the things we don't think about are wreaking unseen harm before they burst into view.

An earthquake triggers a tsunami that floods a thousand miles of coastline, dragging hundreds of thousands to their debris-choked watery deaths. This happened more than once in history, and it could happen again. Giant volcanoes lie dormant until, one day, they don't.

The earth, the seas, and even the air, all contain the seeds of our destruction, for all that we could not live without them.

None of us is safe from the fate that awaits all people. No matter the fortress we erect to keep out all risks, danger lurks within. A twisted ankle on a flight of stairs, a lumpy bit of bread choking off the air in a tight passage, or a tiny clot ending up wedged in the wrong vein, and the end is near to us all.

I guarantee you are up to the task of merely meeting your death. Untold billions before you have done so, of every temperament and ability. Do you think you will somehow fail to succumb when the time comes? Have no worries on that account.

Your gift in being forewarned is as follows: To be reminded of our ultimate fate is to be given the chance to become master of it. Not to prevent the outcome, for that is not the province of any person, but to be ready for it.

What then? Do you complain that life is unfair? That some have long lives and others are cut down in their prime?

Better you learn to live meaningfully for the shortest of times than you live a long and unknowing life. The relative lives of people are all so tiny on the grand scope of things that to worry about a year, a decade, or even a century is to miss the forest for the trees.

Even the mountains are ground down by the passage of time. Nothing made of matter will endure forever. Will you reduce your existence to one of suffering because of fears that one day your suffering will end?

Your salvation lies in the acceptance of the inevitable. When you accept that you will have an end, note that you are not hastening to a premature end. Nor do you need to welcome a thing to be unfazed by its appearance.

Though you cannot control what nature has in store for you, you can control what you think of it. And this you accomplish by thinking about it.

As you contemplate, do not listen to what foolish people say about what things are worth. Though many listen to the incessant noise, few hear or take away the right tune.

The media will give you their daily reminders without fail, but you must never forget they are not trying to help you. Though they try to lead you astray by telling you to worry, you will have no problem dismissing their false fearmongering and taking away the true lesson.

The recitation of tragedy makes you stronger, not weaker, when it falls on ears attuned to reason.

Be well.

Chapter Sixteen

On the Length of Life

If the ticking of the clock spurs us to a frenzy of activity it should not be to prolong our lives but to start living them meaningfully

I seem to have gotten you to swallow the greater portion of my earlier mail, but you have spit out my suggestion that ill health is no barrier to the happiness of a wise person.

"We are far removed from ancient Greece and Rome, where death and destruction lay in wait around every corner," you say. "If they had great cause to reconcile themselves to nasty deaths, that is no longer the expectation or reality for people living in modern times."

We do live much longer lives, I grant you, and are much less likely to be cast into slavery or exile or put to premature death by a tyrant's hand. Too, we have conquered many of the ailments and diseases that plagued our ancestors.

But though we have vanquished tuberculosis, AIDS, and measles in most places, still there are countless means by which we are escorted from the world's stage.

And now that the play numbers several more Acts for most of us, how should we think about those who depart in the early Acts versus those who linger long past intermission to the final curtain call?

I am reminded of a remark attributed to Abraham Lincoln, and for our purposes, it does not matter whether he actually said it or not.

In a discussion about the proportion of the torso and legs to the body, Lincoln was asked to comment on the proper length of a person's legs. His reply: "Long enough to reach from his body to the ground."

It is a gift to be witty when speaking of profound things, dear reader. I make claim to neither wit nor profundity but only truth when I tell you that a person's life should be as long as it lasts.

Is the world a better place when we extend the lives of wicked people? Would we have wanted more of Stalin, Mussolini, or Pol Pot? We need not make examples only of mass murderers to see the validity of this point.

"But this is no argument in favor of cutting short the lives of the good," you say.

True, and you know by now what I will say back to you, be patient with me a moment more.

We hold that the highest attainment a person can reach is to master their reason and live according to the judgment of their well-ordered mind. This wise person knows what is valuable and what is not and acts accordingly.

They are not troubled by superficial things but see beneath the surface. That which is in their control, including their judgment, decisions, and actions, they do control. That which is beyond their control, such as fate, fortune, and external things, they do not let disturb their emotions.

The wise leave these things in peace so that their reason may be left in peace. And because they know their death is inevitable the wise person is not burdened when it comes.

If they are not bothered, who are we to be bothered on their behalf? If we were wise ourselves, we would come to the same conclusion.

"So far you have dealt with the extremes — the evil and the good. What of the great middle, who are neither irredeemable nor perfect?"

I will reward your patience with this answer: The great majority of us knowing that our time is limited seek to extend life when what we should be seeking is greater understanding.

Would you rather live a hundred years in confusion and pain or a week in contented contemplation, knowing the meaning of sufficient?

If the ticking of the clock spurs us to a frenzy of activity it should not be to prolong our lives but to start living them meaningfully.

So I will amend my saying above to be this: People's lives should be as long as it takes for them to start living.

As soon as they have achieved this milestone, they will be satisfied with the length of their lives no matter how much longer they play out their parts.

Be well.

Chapter Seventeen

On Mourning the Dead

When compassion turns into indulgence that does not reflect well on either the recipient or the giver

I had occasion to advise a student who had lost his young wife to cancer. He was looking for condolences but had rendered himself inconsolable, dear reader, impervious to every wise word and helping hand.

There is a point beyond which showing patience and understanding no longer demonstrates compassion but rather turns into indulgence that reflects well on neither the recipient nor the giver.

Thus it was that I told my student the following.

I have been urging you and your fellow students to be mindful at all times, which implies two conditions: That you first be aware of the course of your thoughts, and that you then direct your thoughts to the present moment.

Do not lose yourself for fear of what the future holds and do not dwell on past regrets. This is but the advice to the novice, who has little control over their mind. You are in need of stronger medicine, and because I trust you are ready for a deeper lesson, I will pull back the curtain and expand this thought.

We remind ourselves to live in the moment because most people do not manage to live at all. Whether consumed by anger and resentment over their bad luck or impelled by urges they feel strongly but scarcely understand, by casting about in their thoughts they are cast adrift in rivers of discontent.

You are in such a sea of sadness right now that you do not see it is made of your own false tears.

"False tears," you say. "Do you dare question that my grief is genuine?"

No doubt you had true cause for grief. The loss of your beloved spouse so unexpectedly created a great shock. But in giving such free reign to your grief you have now made a habit of grieving.

What, did you think only pleasures could be made into vices? No, people are just as easily given to turning their worst torments into guilty pleasures.

Whether a sweet indulgence or a personal torture, the root of the vice is the same: Surrendering reason to the free flow of emotions, giving up control, and giving in to the torrent.

This is not true passion, merely the loss of reason. You should take no solace in the loss of your reason, for now, you have not only lost your wife, but possession of your very mind as well.

If you had your wits about you as much as you had your tear-stained handkerchief, you would see more clearly that it is better for your tears to fall quietly and naturally while you are composed.

Just as you should not add to your present troubles by worrying about future troubles, or disturb your present peace by recalling past battles, so you should not amplify your grief by adding to it with lavish displays of sorrow.

Look at you! Weeping and wailing and moping about, as if you are the only person who has ever suffered a loss.

Do you think for a moment that you honor your spouse with your carrying-on? Would she be proud of your displays or turn away in embarrassment?

You like to ride your motorcycle to and from class every day through our crowded city streets. Let's say it was you who was carried off early by a sudden encounter with a city bus. Would you wish for your wife to spend a year in sackcloth and ashes before shutting herself into a nunnery for the rest of her life? Shall her life end because yours ended?

You do your spouse a disservice and demonstrate only selfishness when you dwell without end on what you have lost rather than what you have had.

Your wife has gone to the fate that awaits us all. Did you think that she was immortal, and that death did not have her on the list?

Or perhaps it is that you cannot get beyond the thought that her life could have been longer? Certainly, it could have been, but do you go so far as to say that it *should* have been longer?

Remember, her life could also have been shorter, and it could have been more painful. All over the world, children die of starvation, preventable illness, and war. The cancer wards are filled with infants, but you in your grief rail against the world for striking down an adult in her prime.

Everyone who has ever lived has suffered loss. Some succumb completely and take their own lives. This is the ultimate tragedy because it compounds the ill fate of the world and creates unnecessary suffering rather than alleviating it, which is our highest calling.

Countless more find ways every day to live with their loss. Every type of person can do it, whether young or old, whether ignorant or learned, and has done it, and in every type of situation.

Consider that some 150,000 people die every day. Imagine if this led to hundreds of thousands more people removing themselves from a life of their own volition, forcing their semi-animated bodies through the day with sad faces and drooping shoulders. The earth would soon be filled with zombies. And yet, somehow this does not happen.

Even as thousands are newly thrust into grief this very day, as many more find their way back into the warmth and light of the living. Though it seems impossible to you now, you will survive your wife's death, and you will survive your grieving.

Not only will *you* survive, but your memories will survive as well.

You can begin to relieve your sorrow by calling to mind the good times you shared with your wife. What you had together, Fortune cannot take from your memories: The challenges, triumphs, laughter, tears, and so many silly moments that only you two shared.

If you are forced to bury your happy remembrances, then truly you have buried more than your wife.

To be able to remember your wife with the proper spirit, and truly honor her memory, it is time to leave off mourning and rejoin the living.

Be well.

www.ingramcontent.com/pod-product-compliance
Lightning Source LLC
Chambersburg PA
CBHW060347050426
42449CB00011B/2856